Garfield takes the cake

BY: JIM DAVIS

BALLANTINE BOOKS · NEW YORK

Library of Congress Catalogue Card Number: 82-90219

ISBN: 0-345-30712-7

Manufactured in Canada

First Edition: October 1982

1   2   3   4   5   6   7   8   9   10

GARFIELD EATING TIPS

1. Never eat anything that's on fire.

2. Never leave your food dish under a bird cage.

3. Only play in your food if you've already eaten your toys.

4. Eat every meal as though it were your last.

5. Only snack between meals.

6. Chew your food at least once.

7. Avoid fruits and nuts: after all, you are what you eat.

8. Always dress up your leftovers: one clever way is with top hats and canes.

9. A handy breakfast tip: always check your Grape Nuts for squirrels.

10. Don't save your dessert for last. Eat it first.

GARFIELD!

JIM DAVIS © 1980 United Feature Syndicate, Inc.

© 1980 United Feature Syndicate, Inc.

WOULD YOU MIND EXPLAINING YOURSELF GARFIELD?

JIM DAVIS

11-6

11-5

HOW WELL I REMEMBER THE DAY YOU WERE BORN, SONNY. YESIREE, YOU WERE 5 POUNDS 6 OUNCES AT BIRTH. THAT'S BIG FOR A KITTEN

11-12

I WAS OUT OF TOWN AT THE TIME

THEN HOW DO YOU REMEMBER IT?

I HEARD THE SCREAM

© 1980 United Feature Syndicate, Inc.   JIM DAVIS

TELL ME ABOUT MY YOUTH, GRANDPA

11-13

YOU WERE BORN IN THE KITCHEN OF MAMMA LEONI'S ITALIAN RESTAURANT. YOU FROLICKED IN THE FETTUCCINE, ROLLED IN THE RAVIOLI AND ATE ALL THE LASAGNA IN SIGHT

I MUST HAVE BROKEN SOME EATING RECORDS

NOT TO MENTION A FEW HEALTH CODES

© 1980 United Feature Syndicate, Inc.   JIM DAVIS

SOME FRIENDS OF MINE AND I WOULD LIKE TO DISCUSS THIS DECLAWING IDEA OF YOURS

12-12   JIM DAVIS

THANKS, FRIENDS

© 1980 United Feature Syndicate, Inc.

GARFIELD, I'M SORRY I TRIED TO HAVE YOU DECLAWED. LET'S FORGIVE AND FORGET, OKAY?

JIM DAVIS

BUZZ!

I'LL SETTLE FOR "FORGIVE"

© 1980 United Feature Syndicate, Inc.

12-13

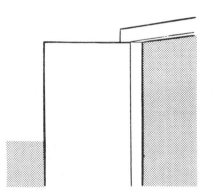

GOBBLE! GOBBLE! GOBBLE!

1-2   JIM DAVIS

WHERE'S YOUR DINNER?!! WHERE'S MY DINNER?!!

GARFIELD

ONCE MY EATING GAINS MOMENTUM IT'S HARD TO SHUT DOWN

© 1981 United Feature Syndicate, Inc.

OKAY, WHO ATE MY SOCKS?

JIM DAVIS

GARFIELD!!

THE GUY'S SOME KIND OF A PSYCHIC!

1-3   © 1981 United Feature Syndicate, Inc.

© 1981 United Feature Syndicate, Inc.

1-23

1-24   © 1981 United Feature Syndicate, Inc.

2-13

JIM DAVIS

SORRY ABOUT THAT

© 1981 United Feature Syndicate, Inc.

GARFIELD! DINNER!

2-14

JIM DAVIS

I APPRECIATE YOUR PROMPTNESS, GARFIELD...

© 1981 United Feature Syndicate, Inc.

BUT, NEXT TIME, OPEN THE DOOR!

OOPS

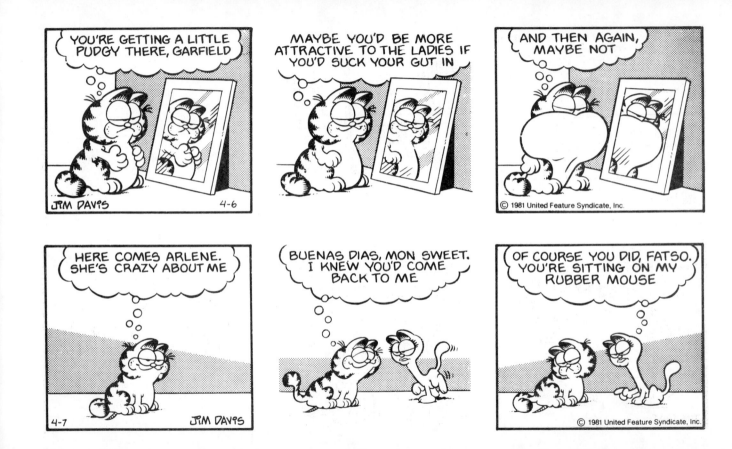

THE MOON IS RIGHT

4-20   JIM DAVIS

THE TIME IS RIGHT

© 1981 United Feature Syndicate, Inc.

GOOD EVENING, LADIES AND GERMS. A FUNNY THING HAPPENED ON THE WAY HERE TONIGHT...

A CANARY WALKS UP TO ME THE OTHER DAY AND HE SAYS, "I HAVEN'T HAD A BITE IN THREE DAYS." SO YOU KNOW WHAT I DID?

JIM DAVIS   4-21

I ATE HIM!

© 1981 United Feature Syndicate, Inc.

YAH DAH DAH DAH DAH DAH

TAPPITY TAPPITY TAPPITY

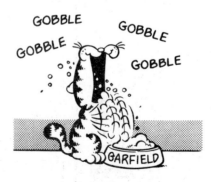

JIM DAVIS

5·6

HOW DO YOU FEEL ABOUT JOGGING THIS MORNING, GARFIELD?

JIM DAVIS

5·7

HOW DO YOU FEEL ABOUT BLEEDING THIS MORNING

I GET YOUR DRIFT

BRIGHT LAD

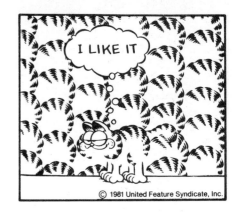

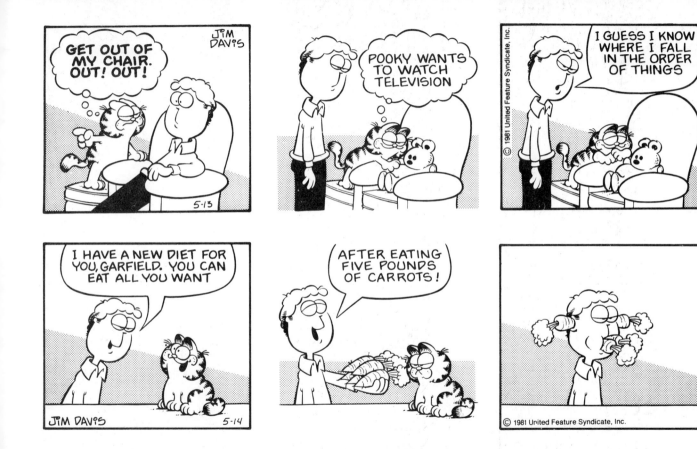

GARFIELD CHARACTERS THAT DIDN'T MAKE IT

When I initially designed GARFIELD, these concepts
never made it off the drawing board. Maybe they could all be
brought back in a strip called ROGUES' GALLERY.

JIM DAVIS